Smoothie

Recipe Book
Ninja

Introduction

Welcome to a delightful world of flavors and health with the Ninja Smoothie Recipe Book!

Authored by the skilled and creative Amaya Williams, this book is a comprehensive collection of smoothie recipes made for your Ninja blender. Amaya, with her expertise in creating nutritious and tasty smoothies, shares her best recipes for you to try at home. Whether you're new to smoothies or an experienced blender, this book is a valuable addition to your kitchen.

Let's dive into the chapters you'll find inside:

Breakfast Smoothie: Kickstart your mornings with these energizing and nutritious smoothies. They're quick, easy, and perfect for busy mornings.

Healthy Smoothie: Packed with vitamins and minerals, these smoothies are your ticket to a healthier lifestyle.

Green Smoothie: Dive into the goodness of greens! These recipes are a great way to include more leafy vegetables in your diet.

Fruit Smoothie: Enjoy the natural sweetness and vibrant flavors of fruit-based smoothies, a hit with all ages.

Protein Smoothie: Ideal for post-workout nutrition or a filling snack, these protein-rich smoothies aid in muscle repair and energy replenishment.

Weight Loss Smoothie: Specially formulated to be low in calories but high in taste and nutrition, these smoothies are great for anyone on a weight loss journey.

Dairy-free Smoothie: Lactose intolerant or dairy-free by choice? These smoothies are created just for you, ensuring no one misses out on the smoothie fun.

Vegan Smoothie: Explore a range of plant-based recipes that are as nutritious as they are delicious.

Detox Smoothie: Cleanse your body with these detox smoothies, made with ingredients known for their purifying properties.

Kids Smoothie: Fun, colorful, and full of flavors that kids love. These smoothies are a great way to sneak in some extra fruits and veggies into your child's diet.

Smoothie Recipe Book Ninja is not just a collection of recipes; it's a guide to a healthier, more fulfilling life. Each recipe is crafted to help with specific health goals like weight loss, detoxification, disease prevention, or boosting energy levels.

The book is user-friendly, with clear instructions and tips for getting the most out of your Ninja blender. Amaya Williams has made sure each recipe is easy to follow, ensuring a pleasant smoothie-making experience.

With recipes for quick breakfast smoothies, post-workout shakes, or fun drinks for kids, this book offers something for everyone. It's time to start making your own homemade smoothies and enjoy the benefits of a healthier lifestyle. Get your book now and begin your journey with homemade smoothies!

Chapters

Copyright

Breakfast Smoothie

Healthy Smoothie

Green Smoothie

Weight Loss Smoothie

Fruit Smoothie

Protein Smoothie

Dairy-Free Smoothie

Vegan Smoothie

Detox Smoothie

Kids Smoothie

Table of Content

BREAKFAST SMOOTHIE

1. BREAKFAST BANANA BLUEBERRY SMOOTHIE

Prep Time: 5 Minutes | Total Time: 5 Minutes | Serving: 1

Ingredients:

- 1 cup frozen blueberries
- ½ cup fresh or frozen baby spinach leaves (optional, but do try!)
- Honey, agave nectar, or stevia, to taste (optional)
- 1 tablespoon ground flaxseed
- ½ to 1 cup unsweetened plain or vanilla dairy-free milk beverage
- ½ cup ice (optional)
- ¼ to ½ teaspoon ground cinnamon, to taste (optional)
- 1 very ripe banana, broken into chunks

Instructions:

1. If you want to add cinnamon, put it in with the frozen blueberries, ½ cup of milk, spinach, seed meal or seeds, and the banana. It will take about one minute to blend until the mixture is smooth.
2. If you want a thinner smoothie, add up to ½ cup more milk. Frozen treats are better when the ice is mixed in.
3. Check the taste and add sugar if needed.
4. Pour into one or two glasses and serve right away.

2. AVOCADO KALE SMOOTHIE

Prep Time: 5 Minutes | Total Time: 5 Minutes | Serving: 2

Ingredients:

- ½ cup ripe avocado
- 2 teaspoon fresh squeezed lime juice
- 2 cups baby kale leaves
- 1 ¼ cup coconut water
- 1 banana, frozen

Instructions:

1. Put coconut water into the blender. Put in the lime juice, kale, avocado, and frozen banana. Put the lid on top and blend until smooth. Pour into two glasses and serve right away.

3. SKINNY PEANUT BUTTER NINJA SMOOTHIE

Prep Time: 5 Minutes | Total Time: 5 Minutes | Serving: 1

Ingredients:

- ½ cup of blueberries & raspberries
- Coconut milk (2 cups)
- ½ cup of strawberries
- 2 tablespoons powdered peanut butter
- 2 teaspoons isolate protein (optional)

Instructions:

2. Using your Ninja blender, blend all of the ingredients together until the mixture is smooth.
3. Put it in a cup, and then sip it on your way to work.

4. NINJA BLENDER BLUEBERRY POWER BLAST BREAKFAST SMOOTHIE

Prep Time: 3 Minutes | Total Time: 3 Minutes | Serving: 1

Ingredients:

- ¼ cup whey protein powder, vanilla
- ¾ cup blueberries, frozen
- 1 tbsp flaxseed
- 1 cup ice
- ¾ cup water

Instructions:

1. Into a Ninja Blender go blueberries, whey protein powder, flaxseed, water, and crushed ice. Make sure the lid is tight on top.
2. Start the blender at its slowest speed and slowly raise it to its fastest speed. This will keep the motor and blades from getting worn out, make the blend more even, and keep food from splashing onto the lid and sides.
3. You should blend for about 30 seconds, or until the mixture is smooth.
4. You can pour it into a glass right away to cool off, or you can put it in the fridge in a container that won't let air in and enjoy it later.

5. OATMEAL SMOOTHIE

Prep Time: 5 Minutes | Total Time: 5 Minutes | Serving: 1

Ingredients

- 1/2 tbsp of pure maple syrup plus additional to taste
- 1 banana chopped into chunks and frozen
- 1/2 tsp ground cinnamon
- 1 tbsp creamy peanut butter
- 1/2 cup of of unsweetened almond milk
- 1/2 tsp pure vanilla extract
- 1/8 tsp kosher salt. Don't skip this, as it makes the oatmeal pop!
- 1/4 cup of of old-fashioned oats or quick oats

Instructions

1. Put the oats in the bottom of a blender and pulse it a few times until the oats are finely ground. Mix in the milk, peanut butter, maple syrup, vanilla, cinnamon, and salt with the banana.
2. Blend until nicely smooth and creamy, stopping as needed to scrape the sides of the blender. If you want the smoothie to be sweeter, taste it and add more sweetener. Enjoy right away.

6. STRAWBERRY OATMEAL SMOOTHIE

Prep Time: 5 Minutes | Total Time: 5 Minutes | Serving: 1

Ingredients

- 14 frozen strawberries
- 1 cup of of soy milk
- 1 banana, broken into chunks
- ½ cup of of rolled oats
- 1 ½ tsp white sugar (Optional)
- ½ tsp of vanilla extract (optional)

Instructions

1. Get the food together.
2. Use a blender to mix the soy milk, oats, strawberries, and bananas until they are smooth. Blend again until smooth, then add sugar and vanilla.
3. Put the liquid in glasses and serve.

7. MANGO OATMEAL SMOOTHIE

Prep Time: 10 Minutes | Total Time: 10 Minutes | Serving: 1

Ingredients

- ¼ cup of of oats
- ½ cup of of frozen mango chunks
- ½ banana, cut into chunks
- ⅓ cup of of plain yogurt
- ½ cup of of orange juice

Instructions

1. Use a blender to mix the orange juice, mango, banana, yogurt, and oats until they are smooth.

8. BLUEBERRY BANANA OATMEAL SMOOTHIE

Prep Time: 5 Minutes | Total Time: 5 Minutes | Serving: 1

Ingredients

- 1 tbsp flaxseed
- ½ banana
- ½ cup of of water
- ⅓ cup of of plain yogurt (low fat)
- Ice
- ¼ cup of of oats (old-fashioned or quick)
- 1 scoop protein powder
- 1 tsp cinnamon
- ½ cup of of blueberries (frozen or fresh)
- 1 pinch nutmeg

Instructions

1. Place all ingredients into the blender and puree until nicely smooth. Enjoy!

9. BANANA AVOCADO YOGURT SMOOTHIE

Prep Time: 5 Minutes | Total Time: 5 Minutes | Serving: 1

Ingredients

- 1 cup of of nonfat Greek yogurt (such as Chobani®)
- 1 avocado, peeled, pitted and diced
- 1 banana, chopped
- 2 tbsp water, or as needed

Instructions

1. Put the yogurt, avocado, and banana in the blender and puree until smooth. Add water to make the smoothie thinner.

10. SPINACH AND BANANA POWER SMOOTHIE

Prep Time: 5 Minutes | Total Time: 5 Minutes | Serving: 1

Ingredients

- 1 large banana, sliced
- 1 cup of of plain soy milk
- ¾ cup of of packed fresh spinach leaves

Instructions

1. Blend soy milk and spinach together in the blender until nicely smooth. Add banana and pulse until thoroughly blended.

11. BANANA GREEN SMOOTHIE

Prep Time: 5 Minutes | Total Time: 5 Minutes | Serving: 1

Ingredients

- 2 tbsp honey
- ¾ cup of of ice
- 1 carrot, peeled and sliced into big chunks
- ¾ cup of of plain fat-free Greek yogurt, or to taste
- 2 cups of baby spinach leaves, or to taste
- 1 banana

Instructions

1. Put spinach, yogurt, banana, carrot, ice, and honey in a blender; blend until nicely smooth.

12. FIG SMOOTHIE WITH DATES AND ALMOND BUTTER

Prep Time: 5 Minutes | Total Time: 5 Minutes | Serving: 1

Ingredients

- 1 tbsp Almond butter
- 4 Figs halved
- 1 Dates can be used 2 if using small dates
- 1 cup of of chilled milk

Instructions

1. Put the almond butter, figs, dates, and Milk in the blender. Blend until smooth. Enjoy immediately.

13. ALMOND BERRY SMOOTHIE

Prep Time: 10 Minutes | Total Time: 10 Minutes | Serving: 1

Ingredients

- water as needed
- ½ cup of of almond milk
- 1 cup of of frozen blueberries
- 1 tbsp almond butter
- 1 banana

Instructions

1. Put the blueberries, almond milk, banana, and almond butter in a blender. Blend until nicely smooth, adding water if you want a thinner smoothie.

14. YOGURT SMOOTHIE

Prep Time: 5 Minutes | Total Time: 5 Minutes | Serving: 2

Ingredients

- 1 ½ tsp white sugar
- 1 tsp milk
- ¼ cup of of pineapple juice
- 1 banana
- 1 tsp orange juice
- ½ cup of of yogurt
- 1 cup of of strawberries

Instructions

1. Put the banana, strawberries, orange juice, yogurt, pineapple juice, sugar, and milk in the blender until smooth.

15. COFFEE SMOOTHIE

Prep Time: 5 Minutes | Total Time: 5 Minutes | Serving: 1

Ingredients

- 1 cup of of milk (plant-based or dairy)
- ½ tbsp of cocoa powder
- 1 cup of of banana (frozen)
- 1 tbsp peanut butter (or almond butter)
- 1 cup of of coffee (brewed)
- 1 tsp vanilla extract

Instructions

1. Put the brewed coffee, frozen banana, peanut butter, vanilla extract, cocoa powder, and milk into the blender.
2. Blend and pulse until there are no chunks left.
3. Before putting the smoothie in, I put some chocolate syrup in the glass to make it look nice. It is unnecessary, but it's a fun finishing touch! Sarve

16. GREEN TEA MATCHA SMOOTHIE

Prep Time: 5 Minutes | Cook Time: 00 Minutes

Total Time: 5 Minutes | Serving: 2

Ingredients

- 1 banana, sliced
- 1 cup of of baby spinach
- 2 cups of ice cubes
- ½ cup of of nonfat plain Greek yogurt or dairy-free
- 1 cup of of baby kale
- 1 tbsp matcha green tea powder
- ¼ cup of of sliced almonds
- 1 cup of of unsweetened almond milk
- 2 tsp of natural sweetener,

Instructions

1. Put everything into a blender.
2. Blend the mixture for 60 to 90 seconds or until it is smooth. If you want the smoothie to be thicker, add more ice. If you want it to be thinner, add more milk.

HEALTHY SMOOTHIE

17. ORANGE CHIA SMOOTHIE

Prep Time: 5 Minutes | Total Time: 5 Minutes | Serving: 2

Ingredients

- 1 tsp of chopped, peeled gingerroot (about one 1/2-inch piece)
- 1 tsp cinnamon, plus more for garnish, optional
- 2 tsp honey
- 1 cup of of unsweetened coconut milk
- 1 tsp alcohol-free vanilla extract
- 2 seedless oranges, peeled and segmented
- 1 tbsp chia seeds, plus extra for garnish (optional)

Instructions

1. In the blender, mix the coconut milk, honey, chia seeds, cinnamon, ginger, vanilla, oranges, and 3 ice cubes on low speed until the ingredients start to come together. Set the blender to high and blend until all the ingredients are mixed well and the smoothie gets creamy. If you want it to be colder, add more ice cubes and blend until it's smooth. Pour into two glasses and, if you wish, sprinkle with cinnamon and chia seeds.

18. ORANGE CREAMSICLE SMOOTHIE

Prep Time: 5 Minutes | Total Time: 5 Minutes | Serving: 1

Ingredients:

- 1/4 cup orange juice
- 1 frozen banana
- 1 orange, peeled and seeded
- 1/2 cup vanilla Greek yogurt
- 1 cup frozen peaches

Instructions:

1. Put everything into the blender and blend until it's smooth. Enjoy right away while it's still cold.

19. IMMUNE BOOSTING GREEN SMOOTHIE

Prep Time: 5 Minutes | Total Time: 5 Minutes | Serving: 2

Ingredients:

- ½ teaspoon freshly grated ginger
- 1 ½ cups Almond Breeze Unsweetened Almondmilk
- 1 ½ cups frozen mix of mango, pineapple, and kiwi chunks
- ½ lemon , juiced
- 1 cup roughly chopped spinach and kale , packed tightly

Instructions:

1. Put the Almond Breeze and spinach or kale in a blender and blend them well.
2. Blend the ginger, lemon, and frozen fruit until it's smooth. Add more almond milk one tablespoon at a time if the smoothie is too thick.

20. STRAWBERRY BANANA SMOOTHIE

Prep Time: 5 Minutes | Total Time: 5 Minutes | Serving: 1

Ingredients

- 1 banana
- 1 cup of of strawberries (150g)
- 1/2 cup of of milk can be substituted with dairy-free milk, orange juice, or apple juice

Instructions

1. Blend all the ingredients until nicely smooth. If you want a different texture, add a little more milk.

21. APPLE STRAWBERRY SMOOTHIE

Prep Time: 5 Minutes | Total Time: 5 Minutes | Serving: 1

Ingredients

- 1/2 cup of of strawberry vanilla, banana, or plain yogurt
- 2 tsp honey
- 1/2 cup of of milk Any kind, we used low-fat
- 1 cup of of frozen strawberries
- 1 apple, cored and peeled

Instructions

1. Mix all the ingredients in a blender for 1-2 minutes or until nicely smooth and creamy. Cold is good.

22. CHOCOLATE SMOOTHIE

Prep Time: 5 Minutes | Total Time: 5 Minutes | Serving: 1

Ingredients

- 1/2 cup of of milk of choice
- pinch salt
- 2 tbsp of unsweetened cocoa powder or chocolate protein powder
- sweetener of choice to taste
- 6 ounce vanilla yogurt (no dairy or sugar, if you want)
- 2 tbsp. Peanut butter (optional)

Instructions

1. Put everything in a blender and blend until the mixture is smooth. Serve, and have fun! To create an even thicker smoothie using a high-speed blender (such as a Vitamix), freeze the milk in an ice cube tray in advance. Once the chocolate has been frozen, mix it with the other ingredients to make a very thick chocolate smoothie.

23. PAPAYA BANANA SMOOTHIE

Prep Time: 2 Minutes | Total Time: 2 Minutes | Serving: 1

Ingredients

- 1/4 cup of of Greek yogurt
- 1 tsp pure vanilla extract
- 1 cup of of milk
- 1 small ripe banana, peeled and sliced
- 1 cup of of ice cubes
- 1/2 large peeled, seeded, and chopped papaya

Instructions

1. In the blender, combine ice cubes, banana, papaya, yogurt, milk, and vanilla; blend until smooth. Transfer to a big glass.

24. VANILLA DATE SMOOTHIE

Prep Time: 5 Minutes | Total Time: 5 Minutes | Serving: 1

Ingredients

- 2 – 3 Medjool dates, pitted (soft and fresh is best)
- 1 medium frozen banana
- 1 cup of of unsweetened almond milk (favorite non-dairy milk)

- 1 tsp vanilla extract
- 4 – 5 ice cubes (or another frozen banana)

Optional add-ins:

- 1 scoop vanilla protein powder
- 1 tbsp nut butter (peanut, almond, cashew, sunflower etc.)

- 2 – 3 tsp cacao or cocoa powder

Instructions

1. Put all the ingredients in the blender cup of of and blend until smooth, which can take anywhere from 1 to 2 minutes, depending on your blender. If you need to, add a splash or two more almond milk, especially if you add protein powder.

25. PUMPKIN PIE SMOOTHIE

Prep Time: 10 Minutes | Total Time: 10 Minutes | Serving: 1

Ingredients

- 1 frozen banana
- 1/2 cup of of pumpkin puree
- ½ cup of of plain or vanilla yogurt
- 1/2 tsp ground cinnamon
- 1 tbsp almond or pecan butter
- pinch each of nutmeg, ginger & allspice
- 1/2 cup of of unsweetened almond milk
- 1 tsp vanilla extract

Instructions

1. First, Put all the ingredients in the blender and blend until smooth. Serve it.

26. CARROT SMOOTHIE WITH GINGER

Prep Time: 5 Minutes | Total Time: 5 Minutes | Serving: 1

Ingredients

- 1 banana previously sliced and frozen
- 1 tsp fresh grated ginger
- 1 cup of of chopped carrots, about 2 carrots
- 1 orange peeled and pith removed
- 1 Tbsp of honey. Use agave for the vegan option
- Liquid as needed: orange juice, milk, coconut water, or water works well
- Optional Add-Ins: turmeric and pineapple

Instructions

1. Prep: Peel and slice the banana a few hours before blending it, then freeze it.
2. Mix together: Add banana slices that have been frozen, carrot, orange, honey, and ginger. Blend if you can, adding liquid as needed (the amount will depend on how juicy your orange is) to get the consistency you want. You can add flavorings like turmeric (powder or fresh) or pineapple if you're going to.

27. PINA COLADA SMOOTHIE

Prep Time: 5 Minutes | Total Time: 5 Minutes | Serving: 2

Ingredients

- 1 cup of of ice
- ¾ cup of of coconut milk
- 2 to 3 cups of frozen pineapple
- 1 Tbsp of granulated or coconut sugar, more to taste

Instructions

1. Mix the coconut milk (stir it first), sugar, pineapple, and ice in a blender.
2. Blend on high until nicely smooth. If you need to, add more milk or frozen pineapple to get the desired consistency.
3. Pour into two glasses and, if you want, serve with fresh pineapples.

28. PINEAPPLE COCONUT SMOOTHIE

Prep Time: 10 Minutes | Total Time: 10 Minutes | Serving: 2

Ingredients

- 2 tbsp coconut
- Toasted coconut, for garnish, optional
- 1/2 cup of of coconut milk
- 6 ounce Greek vanilla or coconut yogurt
- 2 cups of chopped fresh pineapple
- 1 cup of of ice

Instructions

1. Mix the pineapple, coconut milk, yogurt, coconut, and ice using the blender. Mix until it's smooth. Pour the smoothie into two glasses and, if you want, top them with toasted coconut. Serve right away.

29. NINJA BLENDER LEAN GREEN SMOOTHIE RECIPE

Prep Time: 3 Minutes | Total Time: 3 Minutes | Serving: 1

Ingredients:

- 1/2 banana, frozen, sliced
- 1/2 cup pineapples
- 1 scoop Collagen Boost, optional
- 1/2 cup coconut water
- 1 cup ice
- 1/2 cup kale
- 1/2 cup baby spinach
- 1/2 cup mango, frozen, chunks

Instructions:

1. In a blender, put ice, baby spinach, kale, banana, mango, pineapple, coconut water, and pineapple. Make sure the lid is on tight.
2. Start the blender at its slowest speed and slowly raise it to its fastest speed. This will keep the motor and blades from getting worn out, make the blend more even, and keep food from splashing onto the lid and sides.
3. You should blend for about 30 seconds, or until the mixture is smooth.
4. You can pour it into a glass right away to cool off, or you can put it in the fridge in a container that won't let air in and enjoy it later.

30. GINGER NINJA GREEN SMOOTHIE

Prep Time: 5 Minutes | Total Time: 5 Minutes | Serving: 1

Ingredients:

- 1 tsp chia seeds
- 1/2 frozen banana
- 1/8 cup coconut milk
- 1/2 tsp organic matcha powder
- 3/4 cup water
- 1/3 unsweetened cashew milk
- 1/3 avocado
- 1 knob ginger
- 1 cup frozen spinach

Instructions:

1. Put in the milk, spinach, ginger, kale, and water first, and then blend them all together. Before adding the chia seeds, turmeric, and matcha powder, put the fruits in the blender. Serve right away and enjoy.

31. AVOCADO SMOOTHIE

Prep Time: 5 Minutes | Total Time: 5 Minutes | Serving: 2

Ingredients

- 1 ripe avocado, halved and pitted
- ½ cup of of vanilla yogurt
- 1 cup of of milk
- 3 tbsp honey
- 8 ice cubes

Instructions

1. Place milk, avocado, yogurt, and honey into the blender; add ice cubes and blend until nicely smooth.

32. SPINACH SMOOTHIE

Prep Time: 10 Minutes | Total Time: 10 Minutes | Serving: 2

Ingredients
- 1 cup of of baby spinach
- 2 bananas
- 1 cup of of water, or as needed
- 1 lemon
- 1 apple

Instructions

2. Peel the bananas and apples, slice them, and place them in a blender.
3. Wash the baby spinach and put it in the blender.
4. Squeeze the juice of one lemon (or orange or lime, if you prefer) and put it in the blender.
5. As needed, add about 1 cup of of water.
6. Mix until it's smooth, then serve.

33. KALE PINEAPPLE SMOOTHIE

Prep Time: 3 Minutes | Total Time: 4 Minutes | Serving: 2

Ingredients

- 1/4 cup of of plain, non-fat Greek yogurt
- 1 frozen medium banana cut into chunks
- 2 cups of finely chopped kale leaves, with the stems taken off
- 2 tbsp of creamy or crunchy peanut butter (use natural creamy)
- 1/4 cup of of frozen pineapple pieces
- 3/4 cup of of vanilla unsweetened almond milk or any milk you want
- 1 to 3 tsp honey to taste

Instructions

1. Put the kale, almond milk, banana, yogurt, pineapple, peanut butter, and honey in the blender in the order listed.
2. Mix until it's smooth. If more milk is needed to get the consistency you want, add it. Have fun right away.

34. CUCUMBER SMOOTHIE

Prep Time: 5 Minutes | Total Time: 5 Minutes | Serving: 1

Ingredients

- 1 cup of of frozen pineapple
- 1 ripe banana, broken into pieces
- 1 cup of of peeled and chopped cucumber
- 10 ice cubes
- 1 handful of spinach leaves
- ½ cup of of Greek yogurt (or coconut milk)
- 1 tbsp of lemon juice or lime juice (optional)

Instructions

1. Peel the cucumber and cut it up. Add all of the ingredients to the blender in the order given. Mix until it's smooth.
2. Eat it right away or put it in a sealed jar for a day; if it separates, shake it to mix it back together.

35. CELERY SMOOTHIE

Prep Time: 5 Minutes | Total Time: 5 Minutes | Serving: 2

Ingredients

- 2 cups of baby spinach leaves
- 4 medium ribs celery (¾ cup of of chopped)
- ½ cup of of water
- 1 banana
- 1 large green apple
- 1/2 tsp of peeled and grated fresh ginger root
- 1 1/2 (1.5) tsp of fresh lemon juice (half a lemon)
- 10 ice cubes

Instructions

1. Cut the celery into chunks. Leave the peel on the apple and cut it into chunks. The banana should be cut into pieces. Peel and grate or chop the ginger.
2. Put everything in a blender and blend until nicely smooth, stopping to scrape the sides as needed and adding a splash more water if it's too thick. You can drink it right away or keep it for up to a day.

36. CILANTRO SMOOTHIE

Prep Time: 5 Minutes | Total Time: 5 Minutes | Serving: 1

Ingredients

- 1 cup of of water
- 2 tbsp chia seeds
- ¼ cup of of fresh cilantro fresh
- 1 banana
- 1 cup of of fresh spinach
- 1 lime peeled
- ½ inch ginger root fresh

Instructions

1. Spinach, cilantro, and water are mixed until smooth.
2. After that, add the rest of the fruit and blend again.

37. SPINACH PEAR SMOOTHIE

Prep Time: 5 Minutes | Total Time: 5 Minutes | Serving: 2

Ingredients

- 2 cups of spinach
- 1 cup of of milk of choice
- 1 cup of of ice
- 1 ripe banana
- 1 medium-sized ripe pear core removed, skin on
- ½ cup of of plain Greek yogurt
- ¼ tsp ground cinnamon
- Optional add-ins: protein powder, chia seeds, hemp seeds, flax seeds, honey, peanut butter

Instructions

1. Put spinach, milk, and yogurt in the blender. Puree the spinach until it is smooth and there are no chunks left.

38. MINT CHOCOLATE GREEN SMOOTHIE

Prep Time: 5 Minutes | Total Time: 5 Minutes | Serving: 1

Ingredients

- 1/4 Cup of of 2% Vanilla Greek yogurt
- 1/4 Cup of of Vanilla protein powder
- 1/2 Cup of of ice
- 1/4 tsp Peppermint extract
- 1/4 Cup of of Avocado Mashed
- 1 Tbsp Mini chocolate chips
- 1/2 Tbsp Agave
- 1/2 Cup of of Kale firmly packed
- 3/4 Cup of of Unsweetened vanilla almond milk

Instructions

1. Put everything but the chocolate chips in the Blendtec and press the "smoothie function."
2. Stop the Blendtec when there are only 15 seconds left until your smoothie is done, and add the chocolate chips.
3. Blend for 15 more seconds on the "smoothie" setting, then EAT.

39. PEACH BANANA SMOOTHIE

Prep Time: 5 Minutes | Total Time: 5 Minutes | Serving: 1

Ingredients

- ½ banana
- 1 cup of of water
- 1 cup of of spinach
- 1 cup of of frozen peaches
- 1 serving of homemade protein powder is optional

Instructions

1. Blend spinach and water in the blender until smooth.
2. Add the remaining fruit and blend again.

---

40. PINEAPPLE SPINACH SMOOTHIE

Prep Time: 1 Minutes | Total Time: 2 Minutes | Serving: 1

Ingredients

- 2 cups of fresh spinach
- Honey to taste, optional
- 1 scoop of protein powder or ½ cup of of Greek yogurt
- 1 cup of of water or almond milk
- 2 tbsp flax seeds
- 1 small banana
- 1 cup of of frozen pineapple chunks (about 4 ounces)

Instructions

1. Put water, banana, pineapple, spinach, protein powder, or Greek yogurt, and flax seeds in the bottom of a blender. Mix until it's smooth. Taste it, and if you want, add honey.

---

41. KIWI CUCUMBER SMOOTHIE

Prep Time: 5 Minutes | Cook Time: 0 Minutes

Total Time: 5 Minutes | Serving: 2

Ingredients

- 2 whole kiwi
- ½ whole pear (cored and peeled)
- 1 cup of of packed baby spinach leaves
- 1 medium cucumber (deseeded)
- 1 ½ cups of ice cubes
- ½ whole granny smith apples (seeded and peeled)
- 1 medium banana
- 2 tsp Sweetener of choice

Instructions

1. Use cold water to wash every piece of fruit.
2. The Kiwi, banana, apple, and pear should all have their peels removed.
3. Put all of the ingredients in a blender and blend until the mixture is smooth.
4. Put half of the smoothie in each glass.
5. Put any leftover smoothies in the fridge.

42. NINJA BLENDER BERRY GOOD DAY SMOOTHIE

Prep Time: Minutes | Total Time: 3 Minutes | Serving: 1

Ingredients:

- ¼ cup strawberries, frozen
- ½ cup raspberries, frozen
- 1 scoop Collagen Boost, optional
- 1 cup ice
- ¼ cup water
- ¼ cup pineapples
- ¼ cup blueberries, frozen
- 1 tbsp goji berries, dried
- ½ cup plain nonfat frozen yogurt

Instructions:

2. Into a blender go blueberries, pineapple, raspberries, strawberries, plain nonfat frozen yogurt, goji berries, water, and crushed ice. Make sure the lid is on tight.
3. Start the blender at its slowest speed and slowly raise it to its fastest speed. This will keep the motor and blades from getting worn out, make the blend more even, and keep food from splashing onto the lid and sides.
4. You should blend for about 30 seconds, or until the mixture is smooth.
5. You can pour it into a glass right away to cool off, or you can put it in the fridge in a container that won't let air in and enjoy it later.

43. SUNRISE SMOOTHIE

Prep Time: 5 Minutes | Total Time: 5 Minutes | Serving: 4

Ingredients:

- 1 cup kale
- sweetener, If desired; honey, agave, stevia
- ½ cup green tea, freshly brewed and chilled
- 1 cup spinach
- ½ cup frozen mixed berries, (raspberries, blueberries, blackberries, etc.)
- ½ cup coconut water
- ½ cup frozen strawberries

Instructions:

1. Put the kale and spinach into the blender.
2. Put in the green tea and ½ cup of coconut water. Mix the ingredients together until the mixture is bright green and you can only see small pieces of it.
3. Blend the berries into the vegetable puree until you get the consistency you want.
4. That being said, the smoothie will be as sweet as the berries. If you'd like a sweeter drink, you can add some honey, agave, or stevia. Don't worry about how spinach or kale might taste—you can change the amounts to your liking. But I promise you, you won't even be able to taste the vegetables!

44. BLUEBERRY SMOOTHIE

Prep Time: 5 Minutes | Cook Time: 1 Minutes | Total Time: 6 Minutes | Serving: 2

Ingredients

- 1 1/2 cups of frozen blueberries
- 1 1/2 (1.5) cups of apple juice can be substituted for white grape juice, dairy milk, or almond milk
- 3/4 cup of of vanilla Greek yogurt
- 1 banana, halved
- Fresh blueberries and mint sprigs for garnish are optional

Instructions

1. Put the Greek yogurt, banana, blueberries, and apple juice in a blender.
2. Mix until there are no lumps left.
3. Pour into glasses; if you want, top with blueberries and mint.

45. STRAWBERRY SMOOTHIE

Prep Time: 5 Minutes | Total Time: 5 Minutes | Serving: 4

Ingredients

- 1 1/2 cups of milk, any variety
- 1/3 cup of of strawberry jam
- 3 cups of frozen strawberries

Instructions

1. Put the milk, strawberry jam, and frozen strawberries in the blender.
2. Cover the top with the lid.
3. Blend until it's smooth.

46. MANGO SMOOTHIE

Prep Time: 30 Minutes | Total Time: 30 Minutes | Serving: 1

Ingredients

- 1/2 cup of of (120 mL) of milk
- 1/2 cup of of plain or vanilla Greek yogurt
- 1 cup of of diced mango 150 g

Instructions

1. Prep: Peel and cut the mango into small pieces, then put it on a plate and freeze it for about 30 minutes to cool it down. (You could also use mango pieces that have been fully frozen.)
2. Mix together: Blend all the ingredients until they are smooth.

47. BANANA SMOOTHIE

Prep Time: 5 Minutes | Total Time: 5 Minutes | Serving: 1

Ingredients

- 1 cup of of sliced frozen bananas, or about 1 large banana
- ¼ cup of of milk, dairy, almond, oat milk, etc.
- ¼ cup of of Greek yogurt, plain or vanilla
- ¼ tsp vanilla extract

Instructions

1. Put everything into a blender. Blend until nicely smooth, adding more milk if necessary to get the right texture.
2. Serve right away.

---

48. PEACH SMOOTHIE

Prep Time: 10 Minutes | Total Time: 10 Minutes | Serving: 2

Ingredients

- 1 1/2 (1.5) cups of fresh or frozen peaches
- 1/2 cup of of crushed ice
- 3/4 cup of of coconut milk
- 1/4 tsp ground cinnamon
- 1/2 tsp sugar (adjust the type of sugar and sweetness to preference)
- 5 ounces vanilla yogurt

Instructions

1. Combine all ingredients in a blender until nicely smooth.

---

49. PINEAPPLE SMOOTHIE

Prep Time: 5 Minutes | Total Time: 5 Minutes | Serving: 2

Ingredients

- ½ cup of of yogurt (plain or vanilla)
- ½ naval orange (peeled)
- ¾ cup of of water
- 2 cups of frozen pineapple
- 1 medium banana

Instructions

1. Combine the pineapple, banana, orange, yogurt, and water in the blender.
2. Mix at high speed until the mixture is smooth and creamy. If you want your smoothie to be less thick, add more water.
3. Now, Pour into cups of and serve right away.

50. WATERMELON SMOOTHIE

Prep Time: 2 Minutes | Total Time: 2 Minutes | Serving: 6

Ingredients

- 2 ¾ cup of of water
- 3 Tbsp honey
- ¼ cup of of lime juice

- 6 cups of cubed watermelon frozen
- 12 mint leaves are optional

Instructions

1. Combine frozen watermelon, water, lime juice, honey, and mint leaves in a high-powered blender.

51. APPLE SMOOTHIE

Prep Time: 5 Minutes | Total Time: 5 Minutes | Serving: 2

Ingredients

- 8 ice cubes
- ¼ tsp cinnamon
- ½ tsp of vanilla extract
- ½ cup of of Greek yogurt
- 1 ripe banana (room temperature)

- ¼ cup of of milk (or almond milk or oat milk)
- 2 cups of fresh apple chunks (skin on, about 1 large or 2 small apples)
- Optional: ½ tbsp of maple syrup

Instructions

1. Cut the apple up. Put all of the ingredients into a blender and break up the banana. Blend until smooth and foamy, stopping as needed to scrape down the sides. If you want, you can add a slice of apple on top. Serve right away or put in a jar with a lid and store in the fridge for 1 day.

52. ORANGE SMOOTHIE

Prep Time: 5 Minutes | Total Time: 5 Minutes | Serving: 5 cups of

Ingredients

- 1 tsp vanilla extract, store-bought or homemade
- 4 fresh oranges, peeled
- 1/3 cup of of milk (soy, coconut, etc.)

- 1–2 tbsp honey, agave, or the sweetener of your choice, if needed
- 2 cups of ice

Instructions

1. Blend all of the ingredients in the blender until they are smooth. If you want, you can add more ice.

53. CHERRY SMOOTHIE

Prep Time: 5 Minutes | Total Time: 5 Minutes | Serving: 1

Ingredients

- 1 cup of of milk dairy or non-dairy
- ½ cup of of yogurt plain, vanilla or cherry-flavored
- 1-½ cups of cherries frozen
- 1 tbsp of maple syrup or honey
- ½ tsp of almond extract or vanilla extract
- 1 cup of of ice cubes

Instructions

1. Fill a blender jar with ice, cherries, milk, yogurt, maple syrup, and almond extract.
2. Mix until it's smooth.
3. Serve right away.

54. DRAGON FRUIT SMOOTHIE

Prep Time: 5 Minutes | Total Time: 5 Minutes | Serving: 2

Ingredients

- 1 1/2 (1.5) cups of frozen dragon fruit
- 1 medium banana
- 1 cup of of frozen berries
- 1/2 cup of of unsweetened coconut milk
- 2 Tbsp. Dried goji berries

Instructions

1. Blend the dragon fruit, banana, berries, and milk until smooth.
2. You can sprinkle on goji berries or mix them in.Have fun!

55. RASPBERRY SMOOTHIE

Prep Time: 5 Minutes | Total Time: 5 Minutes | Serving: 2

Ingredients

- 1 cup of of unsweetened almond milk
- 1 large banana
- preferably fresh
- 2 cups of frozen raspberries
- 1 – 1½ tbsp maple syrup
- 1 tbsp lime juice

Instructions

1. Put all of the ingredients into a food processor or blender at high speed and pulse until the mixture is smooth.
2. If you want more sweetness, you can add more maple syrup. If the smoothie is a bit thicker than you want, add more almond milk until you get the right consistency.
3. Serve right away.

PROTEIN SMOOTHIE

56. NINJA BLENDER CHOCO NUT BUTTER PROTEIN

Prep Time: 5 Minutes | Total Time: 5 Minutes | Serving: 1

Ingredients:

- 3/4 cup skim milk (or your favorite kind of nondairy or dairy milk)
- 6 oz Chobani 0% Greek yogurt (or 2%, flavored or unflavored)
- 3 Tablespoons unsweetened cocoa powder
- 1 large banana, peeled, sliced, and frozen
- 1 Tablespoon honey, maple syrup, or agave
- 1 Tablespoon peanut butter (any kind you like)

Instructions:

1. Make sure you have a strong blender that can handle the frozen banana. The Ninja or Vitamix is what I like.
2. The list tells you what to put in the blender, and how to do it. Blend on high until the mixture is thick and smooth. To make it taste more like chocolate, I would add one more tablespoon after the first two had been mixed in. You might have to stop a few times to stir or scrape the sides of the blender.
3. If you want, you can drizzle your glass with 1 teaspoon of chocolate syrup and then enjoy!

57. STRAWBERRY BANANA PROTEIN SHAKE

Prep Time: 5 Minutes | Total Time: 5 Minutes | Serving: 1

Ingredients:

- 8 Ounces Milk Substitute - or Milk
- 1 Cup Strawberries
- 1 ½ Scoops Protein Powder - Vanilla, Banana, Strawberry, or Natural Flavored
- 1 Cup Ice
- 1 Medium Banana

Instructions:

1. Mix everything together.

58. PEANUT BUTTER BANANA SMOOTHIE

Prep Time: 5 Minutes | CTotal Time: 5 Minutes | Serving: 4

Ingredients

- 2 tbsp honey, or to taste
- ½ cup of of peanut butter
- 2 cups of ice cubes
- 2 cups of milk
- 2 bananas, broken into chunks

Instructions

1. Get everything together.
2. Put ice cubes, milk, bananas, peanut butter, and honey in a blender.
3. Blend for about 30 seconds or until nicely smooth.
4. Have fun!

59. SALTED PEANUT BUTTER CUP OF OF SMOOTHIE

Prep Time: 10 Minutes | Total Time: 10 Minutes | Serving: 1

Ingredients

- ½ cup of of ice
- 1 tbsp cocoa powder
- Flaky sea salt, for garnish
- 1 tbsp peanut butter
- ½ frozen banana
- 1 cup of of Silk Light Vanilla Almond Milk
- 1 scoop vanilla whey protein powder

Instructions

1. Mix everything but the sea salt until it's smooth.
2. At last, Add a pinch of sea salt before serving.

60. PEANUT BUTTER & JELLY SMOOTHIE

Prep Time: 5 Minutes | Total Time: 5 Minutes | Serving: 1

Ingredients

- 1 cup of of frozen strawberries
- 1 cup of of frozen raspberries
- 1 serving (1-2 scoops, depending on the brand) of collagen peptides, or use your favorite protein powder.
- 3/4 cup of of unsweetened almond milk, plus more as needed
- 1 tbsp all-natural peanut butter

Instructions

1. Add all of the ingredients to a large, powerful blender and blend on high for 1 to 2 minutes or until everything is well mixed. If you think the smoothie is too thick, add more almond milk. It makes 1 smoothie. If you want, you can drizzle the top with more peanut butter.

61. BLUEBERRY COCONUT WATER SMOOTHIE

Prep Time: 10 Minutes | Total Time: 10 Minutes | Serving: 1

Ingredients

- 1 ½ cups of frozen blueberries
- 1 cup of of coconut water
- ½ cup of of yogurt full-fat plain or Greek
- ¼ tsp coconut extract
- 1 tbsp hemp hearts

Instructions

1. Blend all of the ingredients in the blender until they are smooth.

62. CHOCOLATE BLACK BEAN SMOOTHIE

Prep Time: 2 Minutes | Total Time: 2 Minutes | Serving: 1

Ingredients

- 1 frozen banana
- 1 cup of of frozen cauliflower
- ½ cup of of black beans
- 1-2 Medjool dates pitted
- 1 cup of of oat milk or milk of like
- 1 tbsp hemp seeds
- 1 tbsp cocoa powder
- 1 tsp ground cinnamon

Instructions

1. Throw everything into a blender. Mix until it's smooth.
2. Pour into a glass and, if you want, sprinkle hemp seeds on top. Serve right away.

63. SPINACH, PEANUT BUTTER & BANANA SMOOTHIE

Prep Time: 5 Minutes | Total Time: 5 Minutes | Serving: 1

Ingredients

- 1 cup of of spinach
- 1 tbsp peanut butter
- 1 cup of of plain kefir
- 1 frozen banana
- 1 tbsp honey (Optional)

Instructions

1. Put the kefir, peanut butter, spinach, banana, and honey (if you're using it) in a blender. Mix until it's smooth.

64. BERRY KEFIR SMOOTHIE

Prep Time: 5 Minutes | Total Time: 5 Minutes | Serving: 1

Ingredients

- 2 tsp almond butter
- ½ medium banana
- 1 cup of of plain kefir
- ½ tsp vanilla extract
- 1 ½ cups of frozen mixed berries

Instructions

1. Mix the berries, kefir, banana, almond butter, and vanilla in a blender. Mix until it's smooth.

65. CHERRY SPINACH SMOOTHIE

Prep Time: 5 Minutes | Total Time: 5 Minutes | Serving: 1

Ingredients

- 1 cup of of frozen cherries
- 1 tsp chia seeds, plus more for garnish
- ¼ cup of of mashed ripe avocado
- 1 (1/2 inch) piece peeled ginger
- 1 cup of of plain low-fat kefir
- ½ cup of of baby spinach leaves
- 1 tbsp salted almond butter

Instructions

1. Blenderize the kefir. Add cherries, spinach, avocado, almond butter, ginger, and chia seeds, and blend until smooth. Pour into a glass and, if you want, top with more chia seeds.

66. ALMOND BUTTER & BANANA SMOOTHIE

Prep Time: 5 Minutes | Total Time: 5 Minutes | Serving: 1

Ingredients

- 4-6 ice cubes
- 1 small frozen banana
- 2 tbsp almond butter
- 2 tbsp unflavored protein powder
- 1 tbsp sweetener of your choice (optional)
- ½ tsp ground cinnamon
- 1 cup of of unsweetened almond milk

Instructions

1. In a blender, combine all of the ingredients and blend until smooth.

67. BANANA COCOA SOY SMOOTHIE

Prep Time: 5 Minutes | Total Time: 5 Minutes | Serving: 1

Ingredients

- ½ cup of of soymilk
- 1 banana
- 1 tbsp honey
- 2 tbsp unsweetened cocoa powder
- ½ cup of of silken tofu

Instructions

1. Bananas can be frozen until they are firm. Use a blender to mix the tofu, soymilk, cocoa, and honey until smooth. Add the banana slices through the hole in the lid while the motor is running, and continue to puree until the bananas are soft.

WEIGHT LOSS SMOOTHIE

68. FAT-BURNING SMOOTHIES

Prep Time: 5 Minutes | Total Time: 5 Minutes | Serving: 2

Ingredients:

- 1 cup pineapple frozen
- 2 tbsp fresh mint
- dash cayenne pepper optional
- 1 cup spinach
- ½ grapefruit peeled and seeded
- ¼ avocado
- 1 stalk celery chopped
- ½ cup brewed green tea cooled

Instructions:

2. Add the rest of the ingredients.
3. Blend until smooth.
4. Blend green tea, mint, celery, and spinach.
5. Mix it again. Serve cold for the best taste.

69. STRAWBERRY MANGO NINJA SMOOTHIE RECIPE

Prep Time: 5 Minutes | Total Time: 5 Minutes | Serving: 2

Ingredients:

- 1 cup of mango, chunks
- 1 Tablespoon of honey
- 1 cup of strawberries
- 1/2 cup of plain or vanilla yogurt
- 2 cups of pineapple juice

Instructions:

1. Put everything into a blender and blend it until it's smooth. HAVE FUN!

70. CHERRY ALMOND SMOOTHIE

Prep Time: 5 Minutes | Total Time: 5 Minutes | Serving: 1

Ingredients

- 1/2 cup of of frozen sweet cherries
- 1 Tbsp almond butter
- 1/8 tsp cinnamon
- 1 cup of of almond milk
- 1/2 frozen banana
- 1/2 cup of of frozen riced cauliflower

Instructions

1. Put all the ingredients in a blender until the mixture is smooth. Change the amount of liquid as needed to get a smooth mixture. Serve right away.

71. PINEAPPLE WEIGHT LOSS SMOOTHIE

Prep Time: 5 Minutes | Total Time: 5 Minutes | Serving: 1

Ingredients

- 2 scoops collagen peptide powder
- 1/2 banana, frozen
- 1 tsp matcha green tea powder
- 3/4 cup of of fresh spinach
- 1 tbsp coconut flakes
- Juice from 1/2 lime
- 3/4 cup of of unsweetened almond milk
- 3/4 cup of of frozen pineapple

Instructions

1. Put all ingredients into a high-speed blender and mix until the mixture is completely smooth.
2. Pour into a glass and drink right away.

72. BANANA PEACH SMOOTHIE

Prep Time: 5 Minutes | Cook Time: 00 Minutes

Total Time: 5 Minutes | Serving: 1

Ingredients

- ½-1 tsp. Matcha green tea powder (optional)
- 2 Tbsp. hemp seeds
- ½ cup of of frozen peach slices
- 1 Tbsp. salted peanut butter
- 1 small (or ½ large) frozen banana
- 1 cup of of fresh baby spinach leaves
- 1 scoop plant-based protein powder (vanilla) or collagen powder (optional)
- 1 cup of of Silk® OAT YEAH™® oat milk

Instructions

1. Put all the ingredients in a blender with a lot of power and turn it on at the lowest setting. Slowly go up to one-third power for 20 seconds, then slowly go up to full capacity. Mix until everything is smooth and creamy. Pour into a glass and have fun!

---

73. PINEAPPLE GINGER SMOOTHIE

Prep Time: 5 Minutes | Cook Time: 00 Minutes

Total Time: 5 Minutes | Serving: 1

Ingredients

- 1 tbsp chia seeds
- 1 orange peeled
- ½ cup of of strawberries frozen
- 1 cup of of almond milk
- 1 cup of of kale baby
- ½ cup of of pineapple frozen
- 2-inch ginger root

Instructions

1. Put kale, ginger, orange, and almond milk in the blender.
2. Blend on high speed until there are no more leafy chunks and the mixture has the consistency of a smoothie.
3. Blend again after adding the pineapple, strawberries, and chia seeds.
4. Serve right away.

74. CARROT APPLE SMOOTHIE

Prep Time: 5 Minutes | Total Time: 5 Minutes | Serving: 2

Ingredients

- 1 large Honeycrisp apple, cored and quartered
- ½ cup of of ice cubes
- 1 cup of of light coconut milk
- 2 large carrots, sliced (about 1 1/2 cups of)
- 1 medium ripe banana
- 2 tsp minced fresh turmeric or 1 tsp ground turmeric
- 2 tbsp fresh lemon juice
- 2 tsp minced fresh ginger

Instructions

1. Mix the carrots, banana, apple, coconut milk, lemon juice, ginger, and turmeric in a blender. About 45 seconds later, the mixture will be smooth. Add ice cubes and blend for about 30 seconds or until soft. Serve right away.

75. MANGO RASPBERRY SMOOTHIE

Prep Time: 5 Minutes | Total Time: 5 Minutes | Serving: 1

Ingredients

- ¾ cup of of frozen mango
- 1 tbsp agave (Optional)
- 1 tbsp lemon juice
- ¼ medium avocado
- ¼ cup of of frozen raspberries
- ½ cup of of water

Instructions

1. Put water, avocado, lemon juice, mango, raspberries, and agave (if using) in a blender. Mix until it's smooth.

75. STRAWBERRY PINEAPPLE SMOOTHIE

Prep Time: 5 Minutes | Total Time: 5 Minutes | Serving: 2

Ingredients

- 1 cup of of frozen strawberries
- ¾ cup of of chilled unsweetened almond milk, plus more if needed
- 1 tbsp almond butter
- 1 cup of of chopped fresh pineapple

Instructions

1. In a blender, combine strawberries, pineapple, almond milk, and almond butter. Blend until creamy, incorporating additional almond milk as necessary to reach the desired consistency. Present promptly.

77. CANTALOUPE SMOOTHIE

Prep Time: 5 Minutes | Total Time: 5 Minutes | Serving: 1

Ingredients

- 2 cups of chopped ripe cantaloupe
- 1 ½ tbsp frozen orange juice concentrate
- 2 tbsp nonfat dry milk
- 1/2 cup of of nonfat or low-fat plain yogurt
- 1 banana
- ½ tsp vanilla extract

Instructions

1. Put a banana that hasn't been peeled in the freezer for one night or up to three months.
2. Take the banana out of the freezer and let it sit for about 2 minutes until the skin starts to get soft. Use a paring knife to take off the skin. (Don't worry if there is still some fiber.) Make small pieces of the banana. Add the cantaloupe, yogurt, dry milk, orange juice, and vanilla to a blender. Mix until it's smooth.

75. PINEAPPLE ORANGE BANANA SMOOTHIE

Prep Time: 15 Minutes | Total Time: 15 Minutes | Serving: 4

Ingredients

- 12 ounces of a big orange that has been peeled and cut into quarters.
- 1 cup of of coconut yogurt
- 1 pound pineapple chunks, 3 1/2 cups of fresh or frozen
- 2 big bananas, fresh or frozen, peeled
- 1–2 cups of ice cubes

Instructions

1. Employ a food processor to combine all the components until they attain a silky consistency.
2. Add some ice cubes if the fruit in your smoothie is at room temperature. If you add the ice before you've blended the fruit, the blender won't have enough room.

79. BERRY BEET SMOOTHIE

Prep Time: 10 Minutes | Total Time: 10 Minutes | Serving: 6

Ingredients

- 2 ounces, 1/2 of a small beet, 1/2 cup of of chunks
- 3 cups of fresh or frozen mixed berries
- 2 ripe, peeled bananas
- 2 cups of fresh orange juice or coconut water
- 1 small piece of ginger, about 2 tbsp
- 1 cup of of kale leaves with the stems cut off, 1 1/2 ounces
- 1 cup of of ice cubes

Instructions

1. Put all the ingredients in a blender in the order given. Lock the lid and, start the blender on low speed, and work your way up to high speed.
2. In a high-powered blender, blend until smooth, which takes about a minute.
3. Serve it immediately for the best taste, but you can keep it in the fridge for up to a day.

DAIRY-FREE SMOOTHIE

80. DAIRY-FREE LEMON SMOOTHIE

Prep Time: 5 Minutes | Total Time: 5 Minutes | Serving: 1

Ingredients:

- ½ cup dairy-free milk
- 1 fresh lemon, scrubbed
- 1 (8 ounce) container dairy free vanilla yogurt
- handful of ice
- 1 tablespoon fresh ground flax seed

Instructions:

2. Put milk that doesn't contain dairy into the blender jar.
3. Add the lemon zest to the milk in the blender.
4. Remove as much of the pith and ribs as you can when you peel the lemon. Take out the seeds. Put lemon slices into the blender.
5. You can add any sweetener and extras you like (see notes), along with yogurt and ice.
6. Mix until it's smooth.

81. CRANBERRY SMOOTHIE

Prep Time: 5 Minutes | Total Time: 5 Minutes | Serving: 1

Ingredients:

- ¾ cup (75 grams) frozen cranberries , (or fresh cranberries but add a handful of ice too)
- 1 large apple , cored and chopped into chunks
- ¼ teaspoon ground cinnamon
- 1 cup (240 mls non-dairy milk
- 1 small handful (about 2 tablespoons) raw pecans or walnuts , or 2 tablespoons of nut butter (see notes for nut-free option)
- 1 tablespoon maple syrup , or agave

Instructions:

1. Putting everything into a blender.
2. Mix until it's smooth.

82. DAIRY-FREE STRAWBERRY BANANA SMOOTHIE

Prep Time: 5 Minutes | Total Time: 5 Minutes | Serving: 1

Ingredients

- 2 cups of hulled strawberries, fresh or frozen
- 1 tbsp honey
- 1 to 2 cups of orange juice or milk that doesn't have dairy
- 2 fresh or frozen bananas
- Juice of 1 lime
- 1 tbsp ground flaxseed (optional)

Instructions

1. Mix 1 cup of of juice or milk, bananas, strawberries, lime juice, honey, and flaxseed in a blender if you're using it.
2. Blend the ingredients, adding a little orange juice or milk at a time if needed, until the smoothie is thick but still easy to pour. Serve right away.

---

83. COCONUT MILK SMOOTHIE

Prep Time: 5 Minutes | Total Time: 5 Minutes | Serving: 1

Ingredients

- ½ cup of of water
- 1 frozen banana
- ¾ cup of of coconut milk (can be light)
- 2 cups of frozen berries

Instructions

1. Put everything into your blender.

---

84. OAT MILK SMOOTHIE

Prep Time: 5 Minutes | Total Time: 5 Minutes | Serving: 2

Ingredients

- 1 cup of of frozen fruit, I used strawberries and cherries
- 1 frozen banana
- 2 tbsp peanut butter
- 1 ½ cups of oat milk

Instructions

1. First, put all of the ingredients into a Vitamix or high-speed blender. Blend on high until it's completely smooth.
2. Pour into smoothie glasses, and, if you want, top with more peanut butter.

85. ALMOND MILK SMOOTHIE

Prep Time: 5 Minutes | Cook Time: 00 Minutes

Total Time: 5 Minutes | Serving: 1

Ingredients

- 1 cup of of almond milk
- 1 banana
- ½ cup of of strawberries
- ½ cup of of blueberries
- 1 cup of of spinach
- 1 serving homemade protein powder optional

Instructions

1. Spinach and almond milk should be blended until smooth.
2. Blend again and add the rest of the fruit. Stop and scrape the sides down if you need to.
3. Pour into a glass and have fun!

86. AVOCADO BANANA SMOOTHIE

Prep Time: 5 Minutes | Cook Time: 00 Minutes

Total Time: 5 Minutes | Serving: 1

Ingredients

- 1 tbsp lemon juice (optional)
- 1 cup of of loosely packed baby spinach or kale
- Protein boosters: 1/2 cup of of Greek yogurt, 2 tbsp chia seeds, 1 tbsp nut butter, etc.
- 1/2 ripe avocado
- 2 bananas
- ½ cup of of water
- 1 cup of of frozen pineapple chunks
- 10 ice cubes

Instructions

1. Take one half of the avocado's flesh and put it in the blender. Put the pieces of banana and the milk in the blender. Baby greens and water should be added. Mix until it's smooth.
2. Add the lemon juice, ice, and frozen pineapple. Mix once more until smooth. You can eat it right away or store it in a sealed jar for up to two days. If it separates, shake it to mix it back together.

87. CHOCOLATE RASPBERRY SMOOTHIE

Prep Time: 3 Minutes | Cook Time: 00 Minutes

Total Time: 3 Minutes | Serving: 2

Ingredients

- 1 cup of of frozen raspberries, slightly thawed
- 1 ripe banana
- 2 containers (5.3 ounce each) Silk Dark Chocolate Coconut Almond Dairy-free Yogurt Alternative
- 1 Tbsp. unsweetened baking cocoa

Instructions

1. Blend all of the ingredients in a blender on the smoothie setting or until they are well mixed.
2. Pour the liquid into one large glass or two small ones. If you want, you can put fresh raspberries on top. You can drink it right away or put it in the fridge until you're ready.

88. ORANGE BERRY SMOOTHIE

Prep Time: 5 Minutes | Total Time: 5 Minutes | Serving: 2

Ingredients

- 4 ounce coconut or almond milk, unsweetened
- 10 ounce of fresh orange juice
- 1 small banana
- Putting mint on top is optional.
- 1 tsp of lemon juice.
- 1 tsp honey or maple syrup
- 12 cup of of strawberries, fresh or frozen
- 1 cup of of frozen cranberries or any other berry you like. You can use fresh berries, but the sauce won't be as thick.

Instructions

1. Fruit, milk, and juice should be put in a blender.
2. Mix until it's smooth. Put in two glasses.
3. If you want, add an extra slice of orange and a mint leaf to the top. You can save it or use it right away.

89. LEMON SMOOTHIE

Prep Time: 5 Minutes | Cook Time: 00 Minutes

Total Time: 5 Minutes | Serving: 1

Ingredients

- 1 (8 ounce) container dairy free vanilla yogurt
- ½ cup of of dairy free milk
- handful of ice
- 1 tbsp fresh ground flax seed
- sweeteners
- 1 fresh lemon, scrubbed

Instructions

1. Pour non-dairy milk into the blender.
2. Add the lemon peel to the milk in the blender.
3. Peel the lemon and get rid of as much of the pith and ribs as you can. Take out seeds. Add pieces of lemon to the blender.
4. Add yogurt, ice, and any sweetener and extras you like
5. Mix until it's smooth.

90. STRAWBERRY LEMONADE SMOOTHIE

Prep Time: 15 Minutes | Cook Time: 00 Minutes

Total Time: 15 Minutes | Serving: 2

Ingredients

- 1 small pinch of salt
- 1 lemon peel and seeds removed
- 1 tsp lemon zest
- 1 pound fresh strawberries trimmed
- 1 ripe banana

Instructions

1. Remove the leaves from the strawberry. Grate 1 tsp of lemon zest and set it aside. Cut off the lemon's peel and take out its seeds and white, papery pith. Peel the ripe banana and then cut it up or mash it. Put the lemon flesh, strawberries, and banana in the freezer for at least 2 hours to harden.
2. Add the frozen fruit, lemon zest, a pinch of salt, and as many ice cubes as you like to your blender.

91. STRAWBERRY BANANA SMOOTHIE

Prep Time: 5 Minutes | Total Time: 5 Minutes | Serving: 2

Ingredients:

- 2 cups frozen strawberries
- ½ cup water
- 8 ice cubes
- 2 bananas (room temperature)

Instructions:

- Using a blender, blend everything together, making sure the bananas are broken up. Mix until it's smooth.
- You can serve it right away or put it in a jar with a lid and put it in the fridge for two days.

92. VEGAN FRUIT SMOOTHIE

Prep Time: 5 Minutes | Total Time: 5 Minutes | Serving: 2

Ingredients:

- 1 large green apple
- 10 ice cubes
- 1 banana
- 1 cup water
- 1 cup frozen pineapple or mango
- 2 cups mixed berries
- 1 tablespoon fresh squeezed lemon or lime juice
- 1 tablespoon maple syrup, honey or agave syrup

Instructions:

1. Cut the apple into chunks, but don't remove the core. Leave the skin on. Put it in the blender first, then add the banana that has been cut up.
2. Add the rest of the ingredients. Stop the blender and scrape it down as needed to make it smooth.

93. VEGAN MANGO SMOOTHIE

Prep Time: 5 Minutes | Total Time: 5 Minutes | Serving: 2

Ingredients:

- 1 cup Dairy-free Unsweetened Coconut Yogurt - or dairy-free yogurt of choice. The coconut flavor is the best!
- 1 small Banana - fresh, ripe, cut in pieces
- 2 cups Frozen Mango
- 1 cup Unsweetened Vanilla Almond Milk - or unsweetened almond milk
- Healthy addition ideas (pick one only!)
- ¼ teaspoon Turmeric
- 1 piece Fresh Grated Ginger - 0.5 cm, peeled, grated
- ½ cup Fresh Baby Spinach

Instructions:

1. Put yogurt, frozen mango, banana chunks, and almond milk in a blender jug. To give your health a boost, add one of the healthy things suggested in the recipe above.
2. Blend until smooth and thick. If it's too thick or hard to blend, add more almond milk.
3. Serve right away.

94. ANTI-INFLAMMATORY SMOOTHIE

Prep Time: 10 Minutes | Total Time: 10 Minutes | Serving: 1

Ingredients

- ¾ cup of of oat milk
- ¾ cup of of fresh spinach
- 1 cup of of ice
- 2 tsp hemp or chia seeds
- ¾ cup of of chopped pear, skin on
- 2 tsp freshly grated ginger
- 1 tsp honey or maple syrup (optional)

Instructions

1. Put the pear, ginger, spinach, milk, and seeds in a blender and mix until smooth. Put a half cup of of ice and mix until it is smooth and foamy. Taste it to see if it needs honey or maple syrup to make it sweeter.

95. CARROT SMOOTHIE

Prep Time: 5 Minutes | Total Time: 5 Minutes | Serving: 2

Ingredients

- ½ cup of of orange juice
- ½ cup of of frozen pineapple or mango
- 1 large apple, chopped into cubes
- 1 banana (room temperature)
- 1 cup of of thinly sliced carrot rounds
- 10 ice cubes
- Optional mix in: ½ tsp grated fresh ginger, ¼ tsp cinnamon

Instructions

1. Peel the carrots and cut them into thin circles. Keep the peel on the apple while you cut it up. The banana should be cut into pieces.
2. Put everything in the blender, starting with the liquids. Mix until it's smooth. Eat right away, or store in a covered jar in the fridge for up to one day.

96. ACAI SMOOTHIE

Prep Time: 5 Minutes | Total Time: 5 Minutes | Serving: 1

Ingredients

- 1/2 cup of of frozen strawberries
- 1/2 cup of of frozen raspberries
- 4 tbsp of acai powder
- 1 spoonful of hemp seeds
- 1 cup of of liquid, plus more as needed.
- 2 frozen bananas

Instructions

1. Use a blender to mix all of the ingredients together.HAVE FUN

97. KOMBUCHA SMOOTHIE

Prep Time: 5 Minutes | Total Time: 5 Minutes | Serving: 2

Ingredients

- Fizzy kombucha store-bought works, too
- 1 tbsp maple syrup or honey
- 2 cups of frozen fruit
- 1 cup of of unsweetened almond milk

Instructions

1. Put frozen fruit, almond milk, and maple syrup in a blender. Mix until it's smooth.
2. Half-fill two tall glasses with kombucha, then place a scoop of frozen fruit mixture on top and a cherry on top. On a hot summer day, eat it right away.

98. AVOCADO VANILLA SMOOTHIE

Prep Time: 5 Minutes | Total Time: 5 Minutes | Serving: 3

Ingredients

- 2.5 cups of ice cubes
- 1 cup of of unsweetened, plain almond milk
- 1 cup of of frozen riced cauliflower
- 1 ripe avocado, skin and pit removed
- 5 large pitted Medjool dates
- 2 tsp pure vanilla extract
- ¼ cup of of raw, blanched slivered almonds
- 1 large handful of fresh baby spinach

Optional smoothie boosters:

- A second handful of raw baby spinach
- 1-2 tbsp hemp seeds
- 1-2 tbsp chia seeds

Instructions

1. Add spinach, avocado, cauliflower (or zucchini), milk of choice, dates, almonds, vanilla, and any optional smoothie boosters to a high-speed blender. Blend on the highest speed for about 60 seconds or until smooth and creamy.
2. Blend for 30 seconds on high speed with one cup of of ice. Blend again for 30 seconds after adding one cup of of ice. Blend until smooth and creamy again, then add the remaining of the ice. I like to slowly add the ice so that it's easy to mix in. If you want to add everything at once, you can. Then, use the plunger or tamper on your blender to push the ice into the blades. Both ways work just fine.

99. STRAWBERRY WATERMELON SMOOTHIE

Prep Time: 5 Minutes | Total Time: 5 Minutes | Serving: 3

Ingredients

- 3 cups of frozen strawberries
- 1 banana (room temperature)
- 3 cups of cubed watermelon

Instructions

1. Put all of the ingredients in a blender and mix until the mixture is smooth and creamy. Serve right away.

100. CHOCOLATE STRAWBERRY SMOOTHIE

Prep Time: 5 Minutes | Cook Time: 00 Minutes

Total Time: 5 Minutes | Serving: 2

Ingredients

- 1 cup of of ice
- ½ cup of of Old Fashioned oats (optional)
- ¼ cup of of cocoa powder
- 1 cup of of frozen strawberries
- 2 tbsp maple syrup or honey
- 1 banana (room temperature)
- 1 tbsp almond butter
- ¾ cup of of milk of choice (dairy, oat milk, or almond milk)
- For the garnish: 1 sprinkle chopped dark chocolate (optional)

Instructions

1. Put all of the ingredients into a blender and break up the banana. Blend until smooth and foamy, stopping as needed to scrape down the sides and adding a splash more milk if needed.
2. If you want, you can sprinkle the top with 1 tbsp of chopped dark chocolate. This makes a nice mix-in, but it's not necessary. Serve right away or put in a jar with a lid and store in the fridge for two days.

101. BLUEBERRY BANANA SMOOTHIE

Prep Time: 5 Minutes | Cook Time: 00 Minutes

Total Time: 5 Minutes | Serving: 2

Ingredients

- 2 Tbsp Almond Butter
- 1 cup of of Almond Milk (240ml) or other non-dairy milk
- 1 cup of of Fresh Blueberries (150g)
- 2 Medium Frozen Bananas (200g)

Instructions

1. Add almond milk, almond butter, a frozen banana, and fresh blueberries to the blender jug.
2. Mix well until everything is smooth and creamy.
3. Pour into glasses, and then serve right away.

102. GREEN DETOX SMOOTHIE

Prep Time: 10 Minutes | Total Time: 10 Minutes | Serving: 1

Ingredients:

- 1 cup unsweetened almond milk
- ⅛ teaspoon cinnamon
- 1 banana, frozen
- ½ cup pineapple, frozen
- 1 teaspoon fresh ginger, grated
- 1 handful chopped kale

Instructions:

1. Put everything in a blender and blend it well.

103. TROPICAL DETOX SMOOTHIE

Prep Time: 5 Minutes | Total Time: 5 Minutes | Serving: 2

Ingredients:

- 1/2 cup pineapple chunks
- 1/2 mango, peeled and cubed
- 3-4 ice cubes
- 1 cup spinach
- 1/4 cup purified water or coconut water
- 1 tsp grated fresh ginger
- 1 banana

Instructions:

2. In the order given, put all of the ingredients into a smoothie cup or blender. Blend for one minute, or until the mixture is smooth.
3. Depending on the size of the banana, this makes 15 to 16 ounces.

104. KIWI SMOOTHIE

Prep Time: 5 Minutes | Cook Time: 00 Minutes | Total Time: 5 Minutes | Serving: 1

Ingredients

- 1 cup of of spinach
- 1 scoop rice protein powder (optional)
- 1 kiwi, peeled and sliced
- ½ avocado peeled
- 1 peach, peeled and sliced
- juice of a lemon or lime
- Maple syrup to taste
- ¼ cup of of coconut water
- ¼ cup of of unsweetened almond milk
- 1 frozen banana, peeled and sliced
- Grated ginger (optional)

Instructions

1. Put the ingredients in the blender and mix them together.Have fun!

105. ORANGE GINGER SMOOTHIE

Prep Time: 5 Minutes | Total Time: 5 Minutes | Serving: 1

Ingredients

- ⅔ cup of of Bob's Red Mill protein powder (any flavor)
- 2 tbsp Bob's Red Mill Flax Seeds (or flax seed meal)
- ice to taste
- ½ cup of of water
- 3-inch piece ginger (thinly sliced)
- 1 cup of of shredded carrots
- 1 large orange (seedless, peeled)
- ¼ cup of of lemon juice

Instructions

1. Put all of the ingredients in a blender at a high speed and blend until smooth. Add more ice to make it thicker until it's the way you want it.

106. BLUEBERRY DETOX SMOOTHIE

Prep Time: 10 Minutes | Total Time: 10 Minutes | Serving: 1

Ingredients

- 1 frozen banana, cut into pieces to facilitate blending
- 1 cup of of frozen wild blueberries
- 1/4 cup of of water
- 1/4 avocado
- 1 small handful fresh cilantro leaves
- 1/2 cup of of orange juice

Instructions

1. Blend the blueberries, cilantro, banana, avocado, orange juice, and water in a blender until the mixture is properly smooth. Serve at once.

107. APPLE AVOCADO SMOOTHIE

Prep Time: 5 Minutes | Total Time: 5 Minutes | Serving: 1

Ingredients

- 1/2 tsp ground ginger
- 1 cup of of plain unsweetened almond milk
- 4 cups of loosely packed spinach
- 1 medium avocado
- A small handful of ice cubes
- 2 medium apples
- 2 tsp honey
- Optional additions: chia seeds flaxseed, protein powder, almond butter, or other nut butter of choice

Instructions

1. Put the almond milk, spinach, avocado, apples, banana, honey, ginger, and ice into a powerful blender in the order listed.
2. Mix until it's smooth. Try it out and change the sweetness and spices to your liking. Have fun right away.

108. GINGER PEACH DETOX SMOOTHIE

Prep Time: 5 Minutes | Total Time: 5 Minutes | Serving: 1

Ingredients

- 1 orange, peeled
- 1 cup of of cold water
- 1 lemon, peeled
- ⅓ cup of of frozen strawberries
- 1-inch piece of fresh ginger, peeled
- 2 cups of ice
- 2 cups of frozen peaches
- 1 apple, cored
- 1 medium cucumber, peeled

Instructions

1. Mix everything but the ice in a high-speed blender until it's smooth.
2. Blend it again to mix in the ice.

109. SUNRISE DETOX SMOOTHIE

Prep Time: 5 Minutes | Total Time: 7 Minutes | Serving: 1

Ingredients

- 1 medium banana frozen
- ½ cup of of mango frozen
- ½ cup of of frozen strawberries
- ½ cup of of pineapple fresh or frozen
- 1 cup of of coconut water or
- 1 juice of lemon optional

Instructions

1. Use a high-speed blender to blend everything but the ice until it's smooth.
2. Mix it again to incorporate the ice.

110. KALE, PINEAPPLE, AND GINGER DETOX SMOOTHIE

Prep Time: 10 Minutes | Total Time: 10 Minutes | Serving: 1

Ingredients

- 1 banana, frozen
- 1 handful chopped kale
- 1 tsp fresh ginger, grated
- ⅛ tsp cinnamon
- ½ cup of of pineapple, frozen
- 1 cup of of unsweetened almond milk

Instructions

1. Put everything in a blender and blend well.

---

111. SPINACH CUCUMBER SMOOTHIE

Prep Time: 10 Minutes | Cook Time: 00 Minutes

Total Time: 10 Minutes | Serving: 4

Ingredients

- 8 pitted dates
- 1 cucumber
- 2 cups of almond milk
- 1 apple (medium)
- 1 avocado
- 1½ cup of of spinach, packed

Instructions

1. Peel the apple and cucumber and cut them into small pieces. Half the avocado and take out the pit. Cut the dates into chunks.
2. Put everything in a blender and run it until it's smooth.

112. ORANGE CREAMSICLE SMOOTHIE

Prep Time: 5 Minutes | Freeze: 3 hrs | 3 hrs 5 mins | Serving: 2

Ingredients:

- 1 cup soy milk (vanilla)
- 1 (11-ounce) can mandarin oranges in juice
- 1/2 cup yogurt (vanilla, or vanilla soy yogurt)
- 1/2 cup pineapple (frozen chunks)
- 1 tablespoon honey

Instructions:

1. Get the ingredients together.
2. Open the orange can and drain the juice.
3. Put in a plastic bag with a zipper and freeze for a few hours.
4. The frozen pineapple and orange chunks should be put in the bottom of a blender, Vita-Mix, or food processor.
5. Add the rest of the ingredients in the order given. Blend the ingredients together until the texture of a milkshake is reached. If you want, you can add more ice until the mixture is very cold.

113. CHOCOLATE BANANA SMOOTHIE

Prep Time: 5 Minutes | Total Time: 5 Minutes | Serving: 2

Ingredients:

- 1 1/2 cups vanilla soy milk, nonfat
- 2 large bananas
- 1 to 2 handfuls ice
- 1 tablespoon chocolate hazelnut spread, such as Nutella
- 1/4 cup vanilla yogurt, nonfat or low fat

Instructions:

1. Put ice in the blender's base. A handful or two is enough. If you want your smoothie to be more like a juice, use less. If you want it to be more like a milkshake, use more.
2. Add the rest of the ingredients.
3. Blend until smooth. Serve right away.

114. PUMPKIN BANANA SMOOTHIE

Prep Time: 6 Minutes | Total Time: 6 Minutes | Serving: 2

Ingredients:

- 1 tablespoon honey
- 1 cup crushed ice
- 3/4 cup fat-free vanilla yogurt, such as Oikos 0% fat Greek vanilla yogurt
- 1/2 teaspoon pumpkin pie spice
- 1/4 teaspoon pure vanilla extract
- 1/2 cup pumpkin puree
- 1/2 medium banana, very ripe

Instructions:

1. Put all of the ingredients into a blender and blend until smooth. Be sure to crush the ice all the way through.

115. GREEN PEAR SMOOTHIE

Prep Time: 10 Minutes | Total Time: 10 Minutes | Serving: 2

Ingredients:

- 2 tablespoons honey
- 2 to 4 slices fresh peeled ginger, or to taste
- 1/2 teaspoon pure vanilla extract
- 1/4 teaspoon ground cinnamon, or to taste
- 1 cup ice
- 1 medium ripe banana, sliced
- 1 medium pear, seeded and diced
- 2/3 cup almond milk
- 1 1/2 cups coarsely chopped kale

Instructions:

2. Get the ingredients together.
3. Putting the ginger, honey, vanilla extract, ground cinnamon, banana, and pear in a blender is a good idea. Put the ice on top of the kale to make it heavier.
4. Blend until the texture is just right. For some blenders, 2 to 3 minutes may be enough time. To make sure everything mixes well, you might need to stop the blender in the middle and use a spoon to push the ingredients down.
5. Serve right away and enjoy.

116. MANGO PEACH SMOOTHIE

Prep Time: 5 Minutes | Total Time: 5 Minutes | Serving: 2

Ingredients

- 1 cup of of ice
- ½ tsp vanilla extract
- 1 cup of of chopped mango, fresh or frozen
- 1 cup of of diced peaches, fresh or frozen
- 1 ½ cups of almond milk

Instructions

1. Blend almond milk, peaches, mango, and vanilla in a blender. Mix well.
2. Add ice and keep blending until the mixture is smooth. If it's too thick, add a bit more almond milk.

117. MANGO AND GINGER SMOOTHIE

Prep Time: 5 Minutes | Total Time: 5 Minutes | Serving: 2

Ingredients

- 1 tbsp lime juice
- 3/4 cup of of low-fat vanilla or natural yogurt
- 1 Calypso mango
- crushed ice
- 1 tsp fresh ginger (finely grated)
- 1 tsp honey
- 10 ice cubes

Instructions

1. Put two big glasses in the freezer for half an hour.
2. Take the fruit out of the mango and throw away the skin. Put the fruit and the rest of the ingredients into a blender. Blend on high until smooth.
3. Put the liquid in glasses and serve.

118. PINEAPPLE GREEN SMOOTHIE

Prep Time: 3 Minutes | Total Time: 3 Minutes | Serving: 1

Ingredients

- 1 cup of of almond milk
- 2 handfuls fresh spinach
- 1 scoop vanilla protein
- 1 cup of of frozen pineapple chunks

Instructions

1. Put all of the ingredients in a blender in the order given. Mix until it's smooth.

119. CINNAMON ROLL SMOOTHIE

Prep Time: 3 Minutes | Total Time: 3 Minutes | Serving: 2

Ingredients

- 1 cup of of Vanilla Almond milk
- ½ tsp vanilla, optional
- 1 tsp brown sugar, optional
- ¼ tsp cinnamon, plus more for dusting
- 4-5 ice cubes
- 1 ½ frozen bananas, cut into chunks
- ⅓ cup of of old-fashioned oats

Instructions

1. Put all the ingredients in a blender and run it until the mixture is smooth. Pour the smoothie into two glasses and sprinkle cinnamon on top of each.

120. TROPICAL ZUCCHINI SMOOTHIE

Prep Time: 5 Minutes | Total Time: 5 Minutes | Serving: 2

Ingredients

- 1 dash of cinnamon
- 75g frozen banana
- 1 small zucchini, peeled
- 2 large tbs vanilla bean yoghurt
- 75g frozen mango
- 1 cup of of milk

Instructions

1. Put all of the ingredients in a blender and pulse until the mixture is smooth.
2. Put the mixture into two glasses and serve it right away.

121. STRAWBERRY QUINOA SMOOTHIE

Prep Time: 5 Minutes | Total Time: 5 Minutes | Serving: 1

Ingredients

- 2 tbsp low-fat Greek yogurt
- 1 tsp chia seeds
- 1 tbsp honey
- 1/2 tsp vanilla essence
- 130 g frozen strawberries
- 2 tbsp quinoa flakes
- 3/4 cup of of fat-free milk

Instructions

1. Put all the ingredients in a blender and run it until the mixture is smooth.

122. APPLE PIE SMOOTHIE

Prep Time: 5 Minutes | Total Time: 5 Minutes | Serving: 2

Ingredients

- 1 banana
- 1 cup of of milk of choice
- 1/4 cup of of dry old-fashioned oats
- 1/8 tsp cinnamon
- 1 tsp hemp seeds
- 1/2 cup of of ice
- 1 pinch nutmeg
- 1-2 tbsp honey (optional)
- 1 apple
- 1/4 cup of of cauliflower, frozen
- 1 pinch cloves

Instructions

1. Put all of the ingredients into a blender.
2. Blend on high speed for 1 to 2 minutes. If it gets too thick, add more milk.
3. Pour, and give out.

123. CHOCOLATE PEANUT BUTTER SMOOTHIE

Prep Time: 5 Minutes | Total Time: 5 Minutes | Serving: 1

Ingredients

- 1/3 cup of of frozen cauliflower
- 1 tbsp cacao powder
- 1 tsp vanilla extract
- 1/2-1 cup of of milk of choice, regular, almond, hemp, oat, etc.
- 2 tbsp peanut butter
- 2 bananas, frozen

Instructions

1. Put all of the ingredients into a blender that moves quickly.

124. PINK SMOOTHIE

Prep Time: 5 Minutes | Total Time: 5 Minutes | Serving: 3

Ingredients

- 1 ripe banana
- 1/2 cup of of ice
- 2 tbsp honey (optional)
- 1 tbsp hemp seeds
- 1/2 cup of of kefir
- 1/2 cup of of milk – regular, nut, coconut, hemp, etc.
- 1/4 cup of of frozen raspberries
- 1 cup of of frozen strawberries
- ½ – 1 small beet frozen

Instructions

1. Put everything in a high-speed blender. Use the smoothie setting or high speed for one to two minutes or until the mixture is completely smooth. Serve, and have fun!

125. AVOCADO GREEN SMOOTHIE

Prep Time: 5 Minutes | Total Time: 5 Minutes | Serving: 1

Ingredients

- 1/4 avocado
- packed
- 1/2 ripe banana with lots of brown dots
- 3-4
- 2/3 cup of of liquid
- ice cubes
- 1/4 cup of of whole milk plain yogurt
- pinch of chia seeds (optional)
- 1/4 cup of of spinach

Instructions

1. Add all ingredients to the blender.
2. Blend on high for 1 to 2 minutes, scraping down the sides as needed, until the smoothie is smooth and creamy all the way through. The smoothie should be on the thinner side so it's easier for a baby to drink from a straw.
3. Pour smoothie into a cup of of with a straw or a sippy cup of of and serve.

126. GREEN DETOX SMOOTHIE

Prep Time: 5 Minutes | Total Time: 5 Minutes | Serving: 1

Ingredients

- ½ fresh or frozen banana peeled
- ½ Gala, Fuji or other sweet apple,cored, seeded, and cut chunks
- ¾ cup coconut water or water
- ½ cup fresh or frozen pineapple chunks
- 1 cup fresh spinach

Instructions

1. Put all the ingredients in a blender and thoroughly mix until they are smooth.

127. GOLDEN DETOX SMOOTHIE

Prep Time: 5 Minutes | Total Time: 5 Minutes | Serving: 1

Ingredients

- 1/2 cup orange juice freshly squeezed
- 1/2 cup water
- 2 Tablespoons honey greek yogurt
- 1 banana
- 1/2 cup fresh pineapple
- 1 carrot peeled and diced
- ice cubes optional

Instructions

2. Thoroughly mix all ingredients in a blender.

128. KID FRIENDLY GREEN SMOOTHIE RECIPE

Prep Time: 10 Minutes | Total Time: 10 Minutes | Serving: 1

Ingredients:

- 1 medium sized banana
- 1/2 cup diced mango, I like to use frozen
- 2 teaspoons shelled hemp hearts
- 1/3 cup peeled, diced cucumber
- 1/2 cup packed baby spinach leaves
- 1/2 cup unsweetened almond milk
- 1/2 cup diced pineapple, I like to use frozen

Instructions:

1. Blend everything in a blender for 30 seconds to a minute, or until it's smooth. Put it in a mug and drink it.

129. HIGH PROTEIN KID FRIENDLY SMOOTHIE

Prep Time: 5 Minutes | Total Time: 5 Minutes | Serving: 2

Ingredients:

- 2 tbsp peanut butter
- 1 cup milk
- 1 5.3oz cup Chobani Greek Yogurt - Vanilla
- 8-10 frozen strawberries
- 1/2 banana
- 1 cup spinach

Instructions:

2. Put everything in the blender and blend it well. Serve right away and enjoy!

130. SPINACH & APPLE DETOX SMOOTHIE

Prep Time: 5 Minutes | Cook Time: 00 Minutes

Total Time: 5 Minutes | Serving: 1

Ingredients

- ½ cup unsweetened almond milk
- 1 Granny Smith apple (cored and cubed)
- 1 tablespoon flax seeds
- 1 banana
- Squeeze of lemon
- 2–3 cups spinach (packed)
- 1 cup chopped cucumber
- Large handful of ice
- 4 dates

Instructions

3. Put the spinach, almond milk, and banana in the blender and mix until everything is smooth. Add the apple, cucumber, dates, flax seeds, and lemon juice, and blend for 2 to 3 minutes, until the mixture is completely smooth. Blend for another 30 to 60 seconds after you add the ice. Pour into two glasses and add whatever toppings you want. You can eat it right away or put it in the fridge for later.

The End!

Made in United States
Troutdale, OR
05/25/2024